Bones of my Heart

S.A.L.T

CONTENTS

ACKNOWLEDGMENTS

For the one who always believed in me, even when I didn't believe in myself. No matter what I choose to do or not do, you're always there, reminding me that I can figure it out. Thank you, Mum, for always being in my corner, for trusting me when I didn't have a clue, and for just... being you.

For the ones who were there when I needed someone to lean on, My Friends, I owe you. You've listened to my ramblings, sat with me through the silences, and reminded me that even the heaviest days pass.

To the first person who told me my words mattered, My English Teacher. You showed me that pouring my heart onto paper is a way to heal, to connect, and to understand myself. And this book wouldn't exist without you. Thank you.

And to anyone out there carrying a heart that feels too heavy, these words are for you. Thank you for allowing me to share pieces of myself with you.

I hope you find something in these pages that speaks to your own heart, something that helps you feel seen and understood, even in the hardest moments.

ABOUT MYSELF

So, hey. I'm S.A.L.T. It stands for *'Sculpting Art from Living Truths'*. Sounds fancy right!? Yeahh, I know. But honestly, I'm just another 17-year-old kid trying to figure life out. I'm in the end of 12th grade, absolutely clueless about what's next.

People keep asking me what I want to do, what I'm interested in studying next, and honestly? I have absolutely no idea about it.

If I had to sum it up, my full-time job right now is being a family disappointment. I've seen my lowest, and I'm still farming there.

Then there's this love I had, thought it was forever, you know? But turns out, forever's a bit shorter than I imagined. Just typical teen heartbreak stuff I guess.

Writing became my thing when I didn't know how else to let it out. These poems are like the pieces of my heart, spilled onto paper. Well, honestly, it's just me trying to make sense of everything.

So, yeah. This is a poetry collection of a teenager going through this life. But if these poems make you feel less alone, even for a second, then I guess it's all been worth it.

PREFACE

The heart isn't supposed to have bones. It's meant to be soft. But when you go through enough, when love, loss, and pain dig deep enough, you start feeling like maybe it does. Maybe, after everything, even the heart learns to harden, to hold itself up when nothing else will. *(Umm... seems like I've kinda overcooked it, but anyways.)*

But these poems? They're those pieces. The parts of me that refused to disappear, the feelings that turned solid instead of fading away. If my heart had bones, this book would be them.

Bones of My Heart, is a collection of poems I wrote over the span of eight months, after something that felt a lot like heartbreak. I wouldn't call this book an organized collection, it's actually messy, but it's real. But then again, so is our life.

Writing was my way of staying afloat when I felt like I was drowning. Poetry became the space where I could say everything I couldn't out loud, and for that, I'm grateful. I never planned to share these poems, let alone publish them. But people kept telling me they were worth reading, and eventually, I thought, why not let others feel them too?

I had no clue how to put a book together. No roadmap, no structure, nothing, just words that meant something to me. And now, they're here, in your hands.

To you, the one who's reading this, I hope you find something in these pages that speaks to you. I hope these words remind you that whatever you're going through, you're not alone. Somewhere, someone, has felt it too and turned it into words.

This is my first book, and it means the world to me, that you're here, reading this.

Thank you.

She,

She... she was everything I didn't know I needed,
a heart so pure, so untouched, untainted,
like the morning dew on petals, she's unbroken,
her innocence spoke what words had forsaken.
Her eyes are the pools where I found myself
drowned,
it held stories that she never allowed to sound.
In her gaze, I found a place called home,
yet now, I sit in the silence, reminiscing all alone.

Her smile, oh God!!, I used to live for that smile,
it could make my hardest days, worthwhile.
The way her lips curled, that melted my soul,
yet behind it, I knew there was always more to hold.
Her laugh, a song that once healed me whole,
now are echoes, a haunting sound I can't control.
I wonder, does she still laugh that way?
Does someone else get to hear it every damn day?

She never knew how beautiful she was,
her skin, it's a sun-kissed canvas,
her hair was wild and soft as if it was spun
by the hands of a dream, yet to be undone.
Her voice was soft, but it was never unsure,
each word was like a secret I wanted to endure.
I was lucky, blessed, even to be the first
to taste her love, to be in her vest.
But I never thought I'd be the one to watch her go,
to stand in the wreckage of what I used to know.

She loved like someone, who feared breaking,
never too bold, she was always second-guessing.
Her hands, so restless, like her thoughts, never calm,
her heart, fragile but beautiful, just like a psalm.
She'd doodle, tap, fill the silence with a noise,
and in those moments, I saw a little girl behind the
poise.
She never wanted to hurt anyone, never wanted to
fail,
yet now here I am, holding the weight of this tale.

She was truthful to her roots, to her kin,
so loyal, that she was afraid, even to let me in.
She didn't want to disappoint, so she kept everything
inside,
even when it meant to letting pieces of her die.
I was the one, she let slip past her wall,
the boy who saw her when no one saw at all.
But even I couldn't stay in her heart's confined space,
for I became the wrong thing at the wrong place.

I remember the way she'd walk, a little offbeat,
and when with her friend, they'd stumble like misfit
feet.
I always loved those quirks, and the awkward grace,
but now, I long for just one more glance at her face.
She had a love for fantasy, a mind that roamed free,
yet somehow, she couldn't imagine a future with me.
And I guess that's okay, I guess, it has to be,
even though it's killing me slowly, endlessly.

She feared of hurting others, so she stayed quiet,
and let her life make choices, let the world riot.
She couldn't say no, even when it hurt her deep,
and now it's me, it's us, in this wrecked heap.
But I loved her, God, I love her still,
even when she left, even it was against my will.

I thought she was my forever, my always,
but life had its cruel and twisted ways.
She was the right girl, but at the wrong time,
and now I sit here, trapped in this rhyme,
wondering what it could have been
if fate had let me stay within
her world, her love, her grace, her light,
instead of leaving me in this endless night.

But thank you, my love, for giving me the chance,
to be your first in life's relentless dance.
I know someone will love you better than I ever could,
but I'll always be the boy who stood
in the shadow of your leaving, broken but whole,
because you were the first to touch my soul.

And even as I move on, as I must,
there's a part of me that still feels your trust.
You'll find someone who holds you just right,
who soothes every tear, who kisses goodnight.
And I'll be okay, I'll be alright,
but I'll never forget what we had, even when it fades
from sight.

This is going to hurt
not gonna lie, it already does, like a never-ending ache.
But I don't regret even a single moment,
for loving you, was no mistake.
You were the girl who changed me, broke me,
and even though you're gone, you still own me.

I'll heal, but not completely,
because some part of you stays beneath the surface,
quietly.
And maybe that's okay, maybe that's how it's
supposed to be,
because you were the one who made me see
what love could be, even if it wasn't for me.

I Still Remember,

I still remember the way our eyes locked across the room, so vast,
like twin stars destined to meet in the endless night at last,
our gaze was magnetic, pulling us closer without any fight,
didn't need any words, just that one look and everything felt right.

I still remember how we counted down to that interval bell,
like flowers counting on the sunshine, when they're trapped in a frozen spell,
time moved slow, but we were already ready to break free,
and when the bell rang, it was just you and me, feeling the glee.

I still remember how we blushed, couldn't hide it, even if we tried,
just like the first blush of dawn, spreading so far and wide,
every glance was like the sunrise, so warm and bright,
our cheeks were red with that new-found love, that felt so right.

I still remember our conversations, so carefree, as the summer breeze.

Those were like a river flowing through the woods,
weaving between the trees,
our words were the ripples in the current, so gentle yet
profound
carving through the landscape of our hearts, without a
worry to be found.

I still remember the shyness that coloured your face,
so real,
like those first drops of rain that the desert can finally
feel.
Your smile, a hesitant bloom in a desert burning so
hot,
and my words were the rain that made your heartbeat
stop.

I still remember how you couldn't wait to hold my
hand,
like a restless breeze, chasing the leaves across the
land.
We both craved that touch, just like the roots crave
the ground,
and every time we touched, it was something
profound.

I still remember those stories we weaved in our world
of dreams,
like kids living in the wonderland, where nothing is as it
seems.
In our enchanted woods, we were the trees reaching
for the sky,
and our imagination was the breeze that made those

branches fly.

I still remember our first phone call, where you were
shy yet insisted,
like a bird's first song of dawn, so hesitant yet
committed.
Your voice, a gentle melody that surrounds the air
around me,
every word, a new beginning with a promise hidden
there.

I still remember the way your eyes gleamed, like the
moon on the sea,
reflecting a deep ocean of overflowing love, you had
for me,
with a gaze deep and calm, yet crashing currents
hiding underneath,
your glances, a testament of love, even while I was
struggling to breathe.

I still remember the moments when I teased, and you
couldn't keep cool,
like a sudden storm crashing down, bending all the
rules,
but your laugh followed like a thunder that cleared it
all without a stain,
turning embarrassment into joy, like sunshine after the
rain.

I still remember how we stayed up till the night's quiet
end,
like fireflies lighting up the sky, where dreams and

reality seem to blend.
Our voices were the stars, piercing through the
endless grey.
And Our words were the flames, keeping the darkness
at bay,

I still remember the way you felt when I held you
close,
like a willow bending in the wind, soft but still
composed,
our embrace was a refuge from life's relentless
Storm,
a place where nothing could shake us, just us in our
true form.

I still remember the fire in your eyes when others drew
near,
Like a volcano rumbling deep, fuelled by love and
fear,
Your jealousy was a burning flame, so fierce yet true,
A testament to the depth of what I meant to you.

I still remember how your voice shook, when you said
what you felt,
like thunder cracking through the clouds, making
heavens melt.
Your words were the raindrops in a drought, falling so
strong,
dousing the arid land of my heart, showing where they
truly belong.

I still remember your determination in every move and

stride,
like rivers breaking through rocks with a relentless,
powerful tide.
No mountain either high, no valley either deep, can
keep us apart,
our love was a force of nature, burning from the
bottom of our hearts.

I still remember our walks down the hallways, where
time seemed to pause,
like leaves drifting on an autumn wind, with no regard
for nature's laws,
our footsteps, a fragile symphony lingering through our
fading days,
in the dance of life, we desperately wished it would
never drift away.

I still remember the "I love you's" that came from
deep within,
like the first snow of winter, pure, soft, and thin,
each word was a flake, delicate yet holding a world of
truth,
building a landscape of love that could've endured
through our youth.

I still keep your pictures, like flowers pressed between
the pages of time,
their colours might've faded, yet their essence
remains sublime,
as each image a preserved moment, a memory held
tight,
a reminder of the Love we had, that once felt right.

Draft 66,

Lately, I've been saying things that I don't really mean,
just to make this heart break, seem like a bad dream.
Well, I know I should move on, but it feels like I'm
missing you instead,
as my mind is filled with things, I really wish I could
forget.

The scent of your body, it still lingers in the air,
which makes me turn in, thinking you be there,
But all I see is the ghost of our past
blurring my vision with tears so fast.

Yeah, I still remember the way you smiled,
your laugh, your touch, they were so gentle yet wild.
The promises we made and the dreams we shared,
the entirety now haunts me and I'm unprepared.

Those eyes, those lips, everything just pulls me in,
reminding me of what we could've been.
I still have your picture on my phone, hidden,
but I can't bear to see it, knowing that I'm forbidden.

And I'm tired of telling everyone that I wish you were
dead,
'cuz, I can't really hate you, I just hate that you fled.
All I ever wanted was for you to stay,
but I watched as you turned and walked away.

Love?

Love, it is the first light that spills through dark,
it's the silent fire, with a gentle spark.
Not a weight but a warmth, soft and slow,
a quiet touch, a hidden glow.
It whispers close, it pulls you near,
a feeling so vast, you lose all fear.

You dare to touch it, like the rain from the endless
sky,
it's a quiet thrill that won't pass by.
It wraps you like silk, and you hold it like breath,
it fills empty rooms and can defy death.
It's the light in the shadow, bright as flame,
and somehow, you know, it feels the same.

It's a trust unspoken, precious as kin,
a faith so pure, so fierce within.
It's there in the glances and the words unsaid,
it's in the promises made and in paths ahead.
It molds your soul, it makes you whole,
etching its name upon your tethered soul.

They say it fades, they say that it won't last,
but in your chest, it's bound so fast.
It's a dance in the darkness and a song in the light,
A serene morning as well as a star-lit night.
In the silence, in the voice you find,
love becomes sight for the once blind.

The world feels altered, painted with colours new,
each and every shade with a richer hue.
In its embrace, you're brave and bare,
Love is the pulse in the open air.
It's the shared breath, the secret view,
the courage found in something true.

It holds you firm, it holds you still,
a joy so sharp, it's an endless thrill.
Love is the trust that doesn't bend,
the place where everything begins and ends.
It's the breath you hold, the gaze you seek,
a gentle touch that makes you weak.

And so, you let it claim your soul,
filling the spaces and making you whole.
It's fearless here, it's fierce, it's kind,
the softest ache, a steady bind.
It's the silent vow, the quiet call,
it lifts you high yet softens all.

It's every promise that you crave,
the kind of hope you want to save.
It shapes your days, it fills your veins,
a thousand joys, a million pains.
A sacred trust, a lasting thread,
alive in all that's left unsaid.

It reaches to you in every breath,
carving a life from gentle death.
It pulls you close and lets you free,

a pulse, a beat, eternally.
In morning's glow, in starlit skies,
you feel it live; you feel it rise.

It's the endless chance, the leap, the fall,
the boundless faith that catches all.
Love doesn't fade, it grows within,
a path, a song, the light you win.
You live for it, it holds you still,
it's a silent joy, and a gentle thrill.

And when you're lost, it calls you back,
a steady hand through dark and black.
It's the truth you speak; it's the grace you find,
the endless peace that fills your restless mind.
Even raw and bare, it stays the same,
it's like a quiet strength, an endless flame.

For love is the answer, so fierce yet whole,
it's the breath you take, the ache, and the goal.
It's the voice that calls you in every storm,
the light that guides, the touch that warms.
A power so rare, like a boundless fire,
the dream you live, your pure desire.

Love, it's not the kind they paint in a song,
It's not as simple as "right" and "wrong."
It's a feral, bleeding, a brutal embrace,
a haunting ghost that never leaves its trace.
It slips in gentle, like satin and sighs,
until you wake, bound in its lies.

You think it's the light? Uh! Just wait till it blinds,
till it plants itself deep and twists up your mind.
Love's not a kiss, it's a merciless vice,
it's a twist in your gut, a roll of the dice.
You think you know it? well, wait for it, as it's a
maze,
and it'll have you crawling for endless days.

It starts as fingers tracing your skin,
a whisper of hope, a promise of sin.
You think it's soft, till it takes your name,
till it molds your soul and plays its wicked game.
They look at you with eyes so bright,
and hold you tight with a deadly light.

Love is a cage, golden and grand,
where you're left reaching, gasping for a hand.
You want to break free, yet you'll cling tight still,
knowing it's the poison, but you'll be taking your fill.
They're yours, yet not; it's all a lie,
a high that's so low, and you can barely cry.

Their voice is fire, a drug in disguise,
each word a wound, sweetened by lies.
They hold you close, then they let you fall,
they build you up, then steal it all.
Love promises worlds, then shatters your skies,
leaves you craving for what it denies.

You chase shadows, calling it real,
thinking it's the magic, forgetting to feel.
It's the warmth that numbs, the touch that stings,
the wings you're given, then the ground that sings.
For love isn't soft - it's the razor and steel,
it's learning too late what it means to feel.

And then the leaving, oh!! That's the bite,
it's when love fades to dark from dazzling light.
It's the echo of laughter, the ghost in your veins,
their memories etched deep like ancient stains.
You're left with pieces, like a shattered design,
the love you lost, the love that's mine.

But even when gone, it owns you whole,
the hollow ache that carved your soul.
You beg to forget, to purge, to cleanse,
but love's a fever that never ends.
You taste them in words, see them in dreams,
and wake to find nothing is as it seems.

Yet you keep loving them - it's sick, it's cruel,
a never-ending, unbreakable rule.
You're marked by love, scarred and seared,
you'll haunted by faces once revered.
You reach for silence, but it laughs back,
as love's grip, too fierce, its hold too black.

It'll break you down, till all that's left
is the hollow shell of something bereft.
Yet even stripped bare, love finds a way,
creeps back in the night, defies the day.
It's a beautiful chaos, it's the grace and gore,
a cage you can't escape and be begging for more.

Yeah, I know, they say, Love is all you need,
but it's a hunger, an unquenchable greed.
It'll devour you whole, and leaves nothing behind,
yet you'll search for it, blind, stumble to find.
It's the peace and pain, the darkest delight,
it's the poison you drink, night after night.

For love's not tender, it's just ruthless and wild,
it's a burning fire, a demon that once smiled.
You let it consume, to break you apart,
knowing that it'll brand your heart.
And even when broken, you'll come to its call,
because love's the sweetest and the cruellest fall.

Walking through,

It feels like I'm dragging a thousand lifetimes
through the days that all look the same as the prior,
where every step sinks deeper into the weight
of the things I thought I'd left buried deep under,
but find instead sprouting up through the cracks,
clawing their way through bones that forgot how to
heal.

There's a certain rhythm to breaking, you know,
a pulse that whispers truths that I'm not ready to face
yet.
In the quiet, I feel it breathing, this haunting,
not as a shadow but as a presence that wraps around
each thought, like a vine, and it leaves me choking,
tangling into places where hope once used to live.

And hope, uff!! the way it betrays.
It comes like the dawn, soft and silent,
then slips out into the black, laughing,
leaving only the hollow echo of promises I can't
remember making.
I've tried to hold it, clench it tight, but eventually it
slides,
always out of reach, a mirage that dances just beyond
the sight,
a flicker I chase in the empty rooms, leaving me with
nothing
but the weight of all that I hoped to forget.

I talk about peace as if it's my contemporary,
but peace is a stranger with no name,
a quiet that's so thick, presses against my chest,
daring me to breathe.
I imagine standing still, letting it all wash over me,
but this stillness feels like surrender,
like laying down arms in a war where no one comes
back whole.
And I'm scared to be whole,
scared to see the pieces I've kept hidden in corners,
too jagged to hold yet too fragile to discard.

Some nights, I wonder if I'm a ghost,
drifting through my own life,
walking the edges of memories that refuse to die.
I'm haunted by faces and by voices that linger
like smoke that never clears.
I tell myself I'm moving forward, but I'm just circling,
trapped in a maze I built with my own hands,
with walls high enough to touch the sky,
a prison where I can only see the freedom,
and can feel it brushing just beyond my reach.

They talk of healing like it's a place,
a destination you arrive at, your baggage checked,
but healing, it is a war that I wage alone,
a fight against a silence that speaks louder than
screams,
a slow bleed that reminds me that I'm alive,
even when living feels like a punishment,
a sentence I've yet to understand.

I hopelessly march, carrying these fragments,
like a soldier of past lives and half-felt dreams,
hoping that someday I'll understand that
why this path is long, why the weight remains,
why I keep moving toward a horizon
I might never even reach but can't turn away from.

Beneath the Silence,

We share the same roof, yet we live worlds apart,
two souls, like strangers, with their own guarded hearts.
We mind our own business, barely a word shared,
but even in this silence, there's a bond we both dared.

There were days when I hated you, and it's true,
and I know, in your own way, you hated me too.
Yet, despite the divide and the unspoken pains.
You're that man, I wanted to go out with, when it rains.

When days gets heavy, I look up, searching for the light,
in those quiet moments, your struggles, gave me the courage to fight,
you've taught me lessons, without letting a single word,
in our silence, I've seen, I've heard, and I've learned.

And here on this day, I wish you well,
with hopes that one day, you'll be proud of me as well,
for the man that I'll become, you'll finally see,
as you've shaped me in ways unknown, silently guided me.

Happy Birthday dad, our conversations may fade in these halls,
but you'll always be etched deep on my heart's walls.

Drops and its Shadows,

It's half past one, and I'm tangled in thoughts that
won't quiet down.
My mind is an endless loop of memories, each one
cutting deep.
Outside, rain beats against the window, it's heavy,
almost angry.
And I can't help but think, *you would've loved this.*
You, with your love for gloomy skies and the world
soaked in grey.
But I… I wonder would you love it, if you knew
that this same rain is tearing me apart right now?

You'd be happy, probably, if school cancelled
tomorrow,
the way you'd grin, texting me fast with that spark of
mischief,
a spark that felt like it was made for me, for *us.*
I can still hear your laugh, see the way your eyes would
crinkle
when you'd text me, the excitement that pours
through the screen,
as if every little shared moment was a secret only we
could know.
And God, that feeling, it was everything. *We were
everything.*

Do you remember our first phone call? I do, so vividly.
The clouds were thick, a perfect backdrop,
like fate had arranged the scene just for us.

I'd never felt anything so pure, so intense,
like the world stopped spinning
just so we could hear each other breathe,
just so two people could find each other
in a moment carved out by the universe.

And now? Now it feels like a lie. Like something
beautiful
turned bitter, left to rot in a place I can't escape.

And it's around 3 AM now, and it's just me, alone in the
dark, writing
staring at the rain on my window, knowing that the
feeling is gone.
Knowing that for you, those memories mean nothing
now.
And I'm left here with their weight, an unbearable
weight
that presses down harder with every thought of you.
It's like trying to hold onto something that's been
ripped away,
like reaching into the dark and finding nothing but air.

Tell me, was I really that easy to forget?
What did I do that made you erase me so completely?
All I ever did was love you, with every beat, with every
breath,
with a kind of blind, stupid faith that you were my
forever.

I dreamed of our future, sketched it out in pieces and
promises
that I thought we both believed in. We made plans
together,
you in my arms, just us against the world under stormy
skies.
But here I am, in the same rain, and you're nowhere,
you're nowhere, and all I have are the broken pieces of
those dreams.

The way you look at me now,
I can't even bear it. That coldness in your eyes,
like I'm a stranger who somehow wronged you.
I see it every time, that silent wall between us,
and it tears at me in ways I can't explain.

I feel it in my chest, a dull ache, a wound that won't
heal,
like I'm cursed to carry this burden all alone,
knowing I meant so little to you in the end.
I've tried to understand, tried to find some reason,
something to explain how you went from love to hate.

Was I too much? Did I love you so hard
that it suffocated you, left no room to breathe?
Or was it the opposite, did I never really know you?
never see that this was all temporary, destined to
fade?

All I wanted was to build a life with you in it.
But you left me standing in the ruins of something
I thought would last forever, and I don't know how to

let it go.

You've moved on, probably without a second thought.
I bet you don't lose sleep like this, haunted by ghosts
of a love that was real, at least to me.

I'm left clutching memories that burn so bright,
scraps of happiness that feel like a poisoned bite.
It's a cruel irony, don't you think?
That I loved you so fiercely, and now I'm nothing but
just a shadow,
someone you'll barely remember, someone you
resent.
If I could, I'd hate you back. I'd bury these feelings,
make you as small in my mind as I am in yours.

But I can't, I'm not you. I just can't... can't un-feel
everything
we shared, can't erase every promise and every quiet
laugh.
So here I am, hollow and aching, trapped in a love
that's nothing but ashes, a love that leaves me cold
and empty,
while you walk free, untouched by the fire that's
consuming me.

Yeah, just go on. Forget me if you have to, bury every
trace.
I'll stay here, in the rain that won't let me forget,
knowing I loved you harder than I'll ever love again,
and hoping that maybe one day, just once,
you'll remember what it felt like to be loved this way.

I've Failed you,

I'm sorry mum, I've failed you in ways too deep to
name,
a weight I carry in the silence, drenched in shame.
I've failed even as a friend, my bonds are turned to
dust,
the promises are broken, and I lost every trust.

As a student, I tried, but I just can't seem to ascend,
every grade is a reminder of where the dreams end.
The ink on those sheets' bleeds like an old regret,
marking the paths I haven't, couldn't conquer yet.

And as a human, God, how I've fallen short,
a ship adrift in the endless ocean, without anchor or a
port.
I stumble through this life, lost in my own skin,
waging the wars I was never destined to win.

But as your child Mum, this failure stings so deep,
it's a wound that festers when I try to sleep.
You... you poured your love into my every breath,
but I turned it to sorrow, into a quiet death.

I see it mum, in the way your shoulders sag,
the way your smiles sometimes drag.
You don't say those words, but I can feel them loud,
your dreams for me, buried under the doubt's shroud.

I've failed you, Mum, I can see it so damn clear,
your sacrifices are getting wasted year after year.
You worked, you prayed, you gave me the all the stars,
but all I ever did was to turn them into unreachable scars.

Still, I... I try, I swear, I try,
even when the effort makes me want to die.
I claw at the walls, I run toward the light,
but my steps, they all always falter, swallowed by night.

Every goal I set, they just crumble to ash,
and every hope turns to a wound I can't stash.
I stretch my arms, hoping to build something new,
but all I leave is a wreckage, which is unbearable for you.

You gave me the roots to grow tall and strong,
but my branches are twisted, bent, and all wrong.
You gave me the wings to take to the skies,
but I clipped them myself with my failures and lies.

Your sacrifices, they hang like ghosts in this space,
every tear, every line etched on your face.
The nights you stayed up, the dreams you sold,
all for a future I failed even to hold.

And I know mum you're hurt, I... I see your pain,
And also a love so pure, met with this strain.

Your hands are so tired, your spirit worn so thin,
because you... you carry my burdens deep within.

I wanted to be the reason for your smile,
to bring you the joy, to be your child.
But I've only been a shadow, that drags you down,
a crown of thorns where there should be a crown.

I don't know mum if I'll ever be enough,
if I'll rise above this path that's just so damn rough.
But I promise, Mum, I'll keep trying my best,
even as failure tightens its grip upon my chest.

I'll fight, though the battle leaves me torn,
though each day feels heavier than the morn.
I'll keep walking, even when it hurts like hell,
through this desert of failures, this sea of mirth.

Because I love you Mum, more than words can ever
say,
even when I make your skies turn grey.
I'm sorry for being the weight you bear,
for the dreams I shattered, the pain you share.

I don't know if I'll make it, this road is unclear,
But your love, Mum, is what keeps me here.
I've failed, I know, but I'll keep trying,
Even if it feels like I'm forever dying.

The One who...

He was the one who showed you what love could be,
the one who stayed up when you needed to see,
that even in darkness, there's someone who cares,
who bears his pain, but for you, he always spares.
He was the one who stayed, when the nights were long,
fighting his own battles, but for you, he stood strong,
he was the one who chose to stay near,
even when your words cut deep, and seared.

He was the one who accepted you, your past,
and all your flaws yet decided to be steadfast.
Every piece of you, either broken or whole,
loving you deeply, from the depths of his soul.
Even Though he knew that you weren't his forever,
he chose to love you, never saying "never,"
he accepted that one day, you might walk away,
but still, he held you close, every single day.

And Alas, all you ever did was to place the blame,
Well, he took it all, never saying your name,
he wore the weight, just for your own peace,
Letting you go, for your heart's release.
He was the one who gave his all,
even when all you ever did was to let him fall,
he was the one who loved you still,
with a love so pure that nothing can ever kill.

Road to Nothing,

I'm sitting here on the passenger seat, same road,
same dark sky,
watching the headlights stretch into nowhere,
like they're searching for something they'll never find.
The engine hums low, and my parents are talking
about nothing in the front,
their voices blending into the kind of noise you don't
even try to hear.
It's just me back here, staring out the window,
watching trees blur into shadows,
and it hits me, hard and sudden,
how empty this road feels without you.

You were with me last time, not here, not really,
but in my ear, in my hands, in every damn mile.
Your texts came in waves, filling the gaps between the
silence,
and your voice, God, it's your voice
that made six hours feel like six minutes.
It's your voice that made me believe in the idea of us.
And I hate that I still remember every little thing you
said,
every stupid joke you made to keep me awake.
I can still hear your laugh, sharp and perfect,
breaking through the static of my own exhaustion,
telling me I was dramatic for complaining about how
far it was,
but that you'd sit with me the whole way.

You'd tease me, laugh at my stupid questions,
say things like, *"How do you even come up with this
shit?"*
But you'd never hang up. You stayed, always.
You stayed even when the signal cut out,
calling back the second it came through again,
like you couldn't stand the silence, either.
But now? That silence is all I have.

We passed that gas station, the one where I stopped
last time,
just so I could send you a picture of the moon.
You remember that? I called it our moon.
It hung so low, so heavy, lighting up the trees like it
was alive,
like it was something only you and I could understand.
You told me I was dramatic, said I made everything
look beautiful,
You called me a poet, laughed like I was making a big
deal out of nothing,
but you saved that picture, didn't you?
You told me it looked like it belonged to us.
And I believed you.
I thought the sky bent itself for us that night,
thought the world was on our side.
But tonight, I couldn't even look up.
The moon feels dull now, empty,
like it's forgotten who we were.
Or maybe it never cared at all.

We passed that diner too, the one I made a shrine to
us.
I sat there last time, sent you pictures of the menu,
teased you about how I was eating something amazing
while you were stuck at home with leftovers.
You swore you'd steal my foods if you were there,
said you'd make me buy dessert just so you could eat
half of it.

God, I hate that I can still hear you, can still feel the
way your words
wrapped themselves around my tired heart,
made everything lighter, like it wasn't so bad to stay
awake for the night.
But now? Now the thought of going inside feels like too
much.
What's the point of sitting there when there's no one
to laugh with,
no one to share the moment with,
no one to tell me I'm being an asshole for eating
without them?
It's just another stop on a road that doesn't mean
anything anymore.

And the story, the one about Lucifer.
You started it so carefully, like it mattered,
like you wanted me to feel every word you said.
You stopped halfway, said you'd finish it next time,
but next time never fucking came, did it?
You left it unfinished, left me unfinished,
and now it's just another thing I'll never get back.

I'd kill to hear you tell it now,
to let your voice fill the silence again,
to feel like there's still something in this world
that connects us.
But all I have is the hum of the air conditioner in the car
and the ache that keeps spreading through my chest.

And the road, it doesn't stop.
It just keeps pulling me further away from everything
we were,
past the fields we talked about,
past the empty houses with lights flickering in their
windows,
past every place where we dreamed a future
that will never exist.
I thought retracing this path would bring me closer to
you,
but all it's done is remind me of how far away we are,
from each other.

And the worst part?
I still reach for my phone, out of habit,
half-expecting to see your name light up the screen,
to hear your voice cutting through the dark,
telling me to stop being so quiet,
asking me what I'm thinking about.

But the screen stays black,
and the silence presses harder,
like it knows I have no one to break it for me now.

I'm just a passenger now,
staring out the window at a world
that doesn't remember us anymore.

Every mile feels like another piece of me is falling
away,
another reminder that I can't keep holding on
to something that let go of me.

But even as I sit here,
drowning in everything you left behind,
I know I'll keep coming back to this road.
Because some part of me still hopes it'll take me back
to you,
even though I realised that it never will.

I Don't think about You,

I say I don't think about you anymore.
I walk through days that feel deliberately empty,
as if I've learned to ignore a presence
that once defined my every breath.

Yet in the quiet hours before dawn,
when the world softens into silence,
a memory, a mere whisper of a shadow
stirs beneath the surface, as real as
the cool air against my skin.

I've built my days on the promise of moving forward,
stepping lightly on paths I once swore would be free of
your echo.

But sometimes, in the unexpected stillness
of a crowded room or the subtle sigh of a wind
passing through old streets, your image surfaces,
a fleeting brushstroke on a canvas
I believed had been cleared.
It is not loud; it is not overt.
It is a quiet, insistent pulse that reminds me of a time
I thought I had left behind.

I say I don't think about you no more, yet every so often,
in the midst of my carefully constructed solitude,
I feel a tremor deep in my bones,
a silent confession that what was once shattered
still lingers in the cracks of my resolve.

There is a taste in the air, bitter and unexpected,
like ash left behind after a fire that refused

to burn completely, haunting in its persistence.

I have learned to paint my world with hues of resilience
and clarity,
to insist that each day is a chapter of strength and
renewal.
Yet, even as I carve out moments of quiet triumph,
a hidden part of me listens to an unspoken language...
a language written in the spaces between heartbeats,
where the past whispers truths too subtle for words.

It is a truth felt rather than understood,
a secret melody that echoes beneath the surface
of every resolved thought.

I wander through moments that I claim are free from you,
only to find that the absence of your name is not an
absence at all, instead a space filled with the quiet
remnants of what once was.

It is a place where the light of memory and the darkness
of forgetfulness mingle,
creating shadows that flicker with both pain and a
strange, inevitable beauty.

I have learned that some memories, no matter how much
I try to silence them, have a life of their own, breathing
quietly in the gaps of my deliberate indifference.
In the measured cadence of my every day
I carry on as though I have mastered the art of letting go.

I speak of closure and renewal in tones that sound
resolute, yet in the quiet moments, when the world is
reduced to the whisper of my own thoughts,
I catch a glimpse of something raw and undeniable,

a tender remnant of a time when every word,
every breath, was intertwined with you.

It is not a confession made in anger or regret,
but an imperceptible murmur of truth that something
of you still resides in the depths of my being.

I say I don't think about you anymore,
and in the bustling light of day,
I convince myself of that truth with
every step I take away from the past.

But in the soft decay of twilight,
when the world is painted in muted grays and the
boundaries between then and now blur,
I feel the weight of what I have tried so hard to erase.

It is in these moments that the carefully rehearsed lines of
indifference falter,
revealing a hidden landscape where echoes of you
breathe quietly with purpose.

This is not a plea, nor an admission, but a quiet,
relentless reminder that even as I claim to have moved on,
every unguarded moment carries a secret testimony,
a soft, aching refrain that the heart never truly lets go.

And so, in the interplay of light and shadow,
in the spaces where certainty fades into doubt,
I remain, not as a captive of the past,
but as a keeper of its indelible mark,
where every word, every breath,
continues to hold a purpose
too profound to be dismissed.

Watching you Forget me,

I saw you today, but it felt like a dream,
one where I'm screaming, but you never hear me.
You were close enough to touch, yet miles out of
reach,
and I stood there, my heart's shattered, lost in defeat.

You smiled, God! that smile, how it tore me apart,
a smile I once knew, now ripping through my heart.
I held that smile like it was made of diamonds and
gold,
but now it feels distant, and its warmth has grown
cold.

As I'm standing in the crowd, invisible and erased,
while you're living a life where I was completely
replaced.
And the cruellest part of this endless ache
is watching you breathe like it was all just some fake...

I wanted to scream and shout, to break through the
wall,
to remind you of the nights when love was our only
call.
But now those nights feel like stories the old ones
told,
forgotten, discarded, ripped off and left out in the cold.

The silence between us, it speaks louder than the
words,
each and every step you take, feels absurd.
How can you just walk by, like I was never there?
How do you smile when our hearts once shared the
same air?

I've held onto echoes, of the things we once said,
but now they're just ghosts that haunts my bed.
And when I see you, alive in your own world,
I crumble inside, as our memories frantically unfurl.

All I wanted is forever, but what you gave me, an end,
and I'm stuck here, still loving what I can't seem to
mend.
And the hardest part isn't that we fell apart,
it's seeing you, living your best, when you ripped my
heart.

For what Never was,

No, I'm not crying for you, not for the hollowed frame
you left behind,
but for the vision I stitched from broken threads of my
mind.
Not for the face you wore, but the one I painted in the
dark,
not for the fire you were, but the ash I mistook for a
spark.

Do you know what it means to hold a shadow and call
it the light,
to whisper promises to the silence of an endless
night?
I gave you more than love; I gave you the marrow of my
soul,
believing it would fill the cracks in what I could not
control.

But you drank it down like water, and I mistook your
"thirst" for "need",
never seeing the truth, that it was only your hunger I
would feed.
You weren't what I saw; you were the reflection of my
fear,
a ghost wearing the shape of the one I wanted near.

Every word you spoke felt like scripture carved in
stone,

and I was the fool who believed you'd make my heart
your home.
But stone erodes, doesn't it? Truth wears thin,
and the cracks in your voice were the places my doubt
could begin.

You smiled like the sun but left me to shiver in the
shade,
and I didn't see the shadows that your bright facade
made.
I thought you held the world when you reached out
your hand,
but you were only ever reaching for a place to land.

And I gave it to you, my heart, my time, my fight,
until I couldn't tell if the weight of love was worth the
light.
Now the echoes of you are the sharpest kind of lies,
a haunting melody that lingers, though its composer
dies.

I don't grieve for you, but for the song I thought I knew,
a symphony of promises that time could never make
true.
You left me with silence, a wound that doesn't bleed,
a grave where I buried the hope you made me need.

These tears, they're not for the mask you chose to
wear,
but for the phantom I built and begged to care.
They're for the hours I wasted in a house of mirrors
and smoke,

for the weight of every sentence you left unfinished,
half-spoke.
You weren't my salvation, though I called you divine;
you were the altar I knelt at, worshipping a shrine.

And now? Now, I walk through ruins that bear your
name,
each step a reminder of the beauty you became,
not for yourself, but for the dream I wrapped you in,
a mirage of light born from my own sin.
Because it wasn't you I loved, not the way I thought,
it was the comfort of believing I could fix what time
forgot.

Do you feel it, the echoes of the lives we'll never lead,
or do you let the ghosts of us fade as your hunger
feeds?
I'd ask, but I know the answer, know the sound of your
retreat,
how love isn't love when it's the only thing that bleeds.

Remember, I don't cry for you,
not for the empty, not for the shell.
I cry for the heaven I built,
and for the hell I fell.

The Art of Breaking,

What do you call the moment the thread gives way?
a failure of force, or freedom from fray?
Does it mourn its severance, or was it waiting to flee,
a quiet rebellion against what could never be free?
And when it snaps, does it echo in time,
or disappear like a crime buried deep in the grime?

When the earth splits, is it rage or release,
a violent quake or a prayer for peace?
Do the mountains weep as they crumble to sand,
or do they dream of being held in the sea's hand?
Is breaking destruction, or is it rebirth,
a grave for the old, or the scream of new earth?

Does the flame curse the wick for burning away,
or does it embrace the ash, unafraid of decay?
When the fire consumes, is it greed or grace,
a devouring force or a cleansing space?
Does it die with regret for the warmth it gave,
or rejoice in the shadows it taught to be brave?

When the glass shatters, does it cry in despair,
or does it finally exhale, relieved of the care?
Is each shard a wound, or a new piece of art,
a fragment of pain or a freshly drawn start?
And do the hands that bleed on its jagged edge
curse the moment they reached for what was
pledged?

What is breaking if not love's cruel decree,
binding what was and what cannot be?
Do we hold tighter as the cracks run wide,
or let go and fall, breaking alongside?
Does the heart despise the weight it holds,
or is breaking the story it longs to be told?

When the leaves descend, do they grieve their flight,
or do they thank the wind for their brief delight?
Does the tree ache for what it has shed,
or does it find peace in the silence instead?
Is letting go a curse, or is it grace,
a fleeting goodbye or a sacred embrace?

Does the river rage as it bends and breaks,
or does it trust the path the earth remakes?
When the current tears through the jagged stone,
is it destruction, or is it finding a home?
Does it resent the force that carves its skin,
or is breaking the proof of the life within?

When silence is broken, does it scream or sigh,
a burst of chaos or a breath before the cry?
Does it mourn the stillness that will never return,
or does it find itself in the noise it learns?
Is it rupture or release, a fracture or a start,
a violent pull, or the softest art?

Breaking isn't just the moment of fall -
it's the echo, the shadow, the weight of it all.
It's the hand that lets go and the one that still clings,

the fracture that tears and the freedom it brings.
It's the mirror's cracks and the light they reveal,
the rawness of wounds that refuse to heal.

It's the star collapsing under its weight,
a tragedy written as though by fate.
Does it burn in shame as it fades to dust,
or does it trust in the heavens, knowing it must?
Does its end mark loss, or does it ignite,
a spark of creation hidden in the night?

And what of us, when we break and fall?
Do we rise from the rubble, or do we crawl?
Do we find the beauty in being undone,
or curse the shadows for blocking the sun?
Is breaking the moment we lose control,
or the only way to finally be whole?

So, tell me, as the pieces scatter and stray:
Is breaking a death, or the price we pay?
When the world splits beneath your trembling feet,
is it defeat, or the place where you meet
your truest self, raw and bare,
stripped of the lies you no longer wear?

The art of breaking isn't just in the fall;
it's the breath that lingers, the voice that calls.
It's the silent question, the ache, the release,
the chaos of pain, the whisper of peace.
It's the beauty of endings, the scars that remain,
the art of breaking - where we're reborn from the pain.

What is Love but a Wound that Never Heals?

What is love but the sharpest of blades,
a promise dressed in the finest charades?
It cuts you clean, it digs so deep,
it's a wound you cradle but never keep.
Does it laugh as it carves through your tender bone,
leaving you to bleed out, utterly alone?

What is love but a cruel masquerade,
a beautiful lie that time can't evade?
Is it the weight of a touch that turned ghost,
or the echo of words that haunt the most?
Does it hide in the corners of shattered trust,
turning hearts to ruins, and dreams to dust?

What is love when it whispers and lies,
when it's born in the gaze but dies in the eyes?
Does it curl in the hollow of forgotten prayers,
or linger in rooms where no one dares?
Is it the memory of a hand once near,
now, a phantom that drips like poison in your ear?

What is love when it chose to walk away,
When it doesn't explain, it doesn't stay?
Does it sink like a stone in the pit of your chest,
or burn like a fire that sees no rest?
Is it the silence that grows like a storm,
a rage that keeps you cold, not warm?

What is love when it teaches to hurt,
when it grinds you down, drags your face in the dirt?
Does it wear the face of an old regret,
or a smile that you wish you could forget?
Is it the taste of names you can't unlearn,
each syllable a dagger, each vowel a burn?

What is love but a mirror that shatters,
a reflection that mocks while your heart splatters?
Does it cradle your ribs in a deathly embrace,
or leave you gasping in its empty space?
Is it the weight of nights where you begged the sky,
or mornings where you woke just to ask, "Why?"

What is love but a thief in disguise,
robbing the very colours from your skies?
Does it leave with the sun, take the rain,
turn joy into relics, pleasure to pain?
Is it the scream you choke on while you smile,
the slow decay that aches for miles?

What is love when it no longer stays,
when it turns all your light into shades of grey?
Is it the bruise you press to feel alive,
or the drowning you fight to survive?
Does it hum in the silence after a storm,
a hymn of grief in its softest form?

What is love but the weight of a name,
etched in a language of heartbreak and flame?
You wear it like a charm, though it makes you fall,
and you'd still kneel, still crawl, still give it all.
For love is a god that devours its own,
leaving you worshipping on an empty throne.

And yet, you'll beg, won't you? You'll pray.
You'll sell your soul just to feel it stay.
For love is a wound that never closes,
a field of thorns that once grew roses.
It kills you slow, it pulls you apart,
but you'll still call it home, deep in your heart.

A Life We Never Lived,

Need? What's needed, baby, if not a life with you?
Not the flashy and loud kind,
but one so simple and holy.
Us, growing old, weathered by time.

A house tucked into a quiet corner of the countryside,
not big, but ours. Walls that carried our laughter,
our arguments, our love pressed into every beam,
every inch of the floor we'd walked a million times.

A backyard that smelled of autumn leaves and
summer's ripe afternoons. Our little piece of the
world, a patch of green where we'd plant dreams.
And in the middle of it all, Our daughter.

God, babe, she'd have been ours,
but you know what I mean when I say,
she was more mine than anything.
Her tiny body curled into my chest,
her heartbeat drumming softly into mine
as she slept in that baby carrier strapped to me.

We'd walk like that, me and her, and you beside us,
to the supermarket down the street on Saturdays.
The sky would blush with sunset
as we filled our bags with things we didn't need.
It'll be heavy with groceries, but not as heavy
as the love we carried back home with us.

And yeah, I'd want a husky, even though
I'd hear you groan about it every time.
"Why a dog?" you'd say, and I'd laugh, kiss your
forehead, and remind you,
"Our baby needs a companion, you stupid peanut."
You'd roll your eyes. But secretly, I'd see it, the way
you'd soften, when the dog's eyes mirrored hers,
Both of them so full of trust.

I'd teach her everything I could, how to swim
through the tides of life, to float,
even when the weight was unbearable.
How to hold patience in her palm
like a fragile flower and let it wither
only when absolutely necessary.
I'd teach her to question the world
and the answers she'd been handed,
to find her own truths,
and build a home within herself.

And faith, she'd have both mine and yours.
Temple bells on one day, Church hymns on another.
Her small hands folded in prayer,
not to divide, but to unite.
Because love doesn't care where it prays,
it just prays to belong.

We'd have a car, nothing fancy, but enough to hold us,
enough to carry the weight of our little world.
Its seats, stained with crayons, the faint scent of
porridge spills and your perfume,
lingering in the air like a memory that never faded.

Mornings, the three of us would pile in,
you in the passenger seat, checking your schedule,
Me driving, and her in the back, swinging her legs
and talking about nothing and everything.

We'd drop you off first, your clinic in the city
gleaming in the soft morning light,
a place where you healed and mended
the world in your quiet way.
I'd watch you step out,
your bag slung over your shoulder,
your hand holding the door frame
as you bent to kiss her.

"Don't be late," you'd say,
but your smile always betrayed you,
soft and lingering,
like a secret only I knew.

Then it was just me and her,
her voice filling the car with questions,
her laughter spilling into every silence.
We'd head to school, where I'd teach words
and dreams to restless minds,
and she'd learn to navigate her own.

By the time we returned,
the sun would be dipping low,
and there you'd be, waiting in the courtyard
of your clinic, your face tired,
but alight when you saw us.

She'd rush to you, her arms flung wide,
and I'd follow, slower,
knowing that my world stood right there,
in the glow of the evening light.

And we'd drive home together,
the three of us again,
the car humming with stories of the day,
her giggles punctuating the air,
as your hand found mine on the gear shift.

The evenings were ours,
as we'd get home together, the three of us,
stepping into the warmth of our little world.
You'd kick off your shoes by the door,
your bag slumping into the corner,
and she'd toss her school bag onto the couch,
already complaining about homework.

But the dinner was ours to share,
you and me in the kitchen,
the clatter of pans, the hum of the stove,
as we worked in quiet rhythm.
I'd chop while you stirred,
or maybe it was the other way around,
we didn't care, because this was us.

While she'd sit at the table, books sprawled open,
pencil tapping against her cheek
as she wrestled with equations and spelling lists.
We'd pause, leaning over her shoulder,

our voices blending as we helped her
to solve the puzzles of her little world.

Her laughter would spill out when we got it wrong,
and her eyes would gleam with pride
when she got it right.
When dinner was ready, we'd all gather,
plates full, hearts fuller.
Her favourite cartoon playing softly in the background.
Sometimes, it'd be her show.
Other nights, it'd be ours.
But no matter what was on the screen,
it was the love between us that played the loudest.

At night, I'd sleep on the floor,
close to you both, watching the rise
and fall of your breaths. My heart, so full it hurt,
as I told myself, *"This is enough. This is everything."*

At 2:30 in the morning,
when both of my worlds are sound asleep,
I'd wake, the stillness thick and comforting,
The kind of quiet that lets thoughts breathe.
I'd slip out of my bed made of bedsheets,
careful not to disturb you both,
and there on the same floor,
I'd stretch and begin the day no one else saw.

First, I'd plan the Lessons for restless minds at school,
then thoughts for the book that lived inside my chest,
words spilling onto the page like whispers in the dark.

The scratching of the pen against paper
would be broken only by the soft clatter
of kibble as I fed our husky,
its eyes watching me with silent trust.

By 4:00, I'd gently wake you,
your face soft with sleep, still tangled in dreams,
eyes heavy with the night.
You'd mumble for your drink,
your voice thick with slumber,
as I mention that I'm gonna make mine.

But I'd remind you,
"Not yet, dummy, not before you brush first."
You'd sigh, but you'd agree, because you knew that
was how we worked, a little patience, a little push,
before the comfort of that drink you craved.
And I'd smile, watching you move slowly.

Then, I'd brew the drinks,
a cup of coffee just the way you liked it,
dark, smooth, a little sweet.
And tea for myself, strong and earthy,
the kind that kept me grounded
through the whirlwind of the day.

And we'd walk outside together.
Just the two of us, the cold air wrapping around us
as we made our rounds through the plot of land
that held our dreams.

Our husky would stay behind, its duty clear,
to guard our daughter's dreams,
to watch over the most precious piece of our world.

By 5:00, we'd be back,
the sunrise hinting at the day ahead.
You'd dive into your own tasks,
while I'd tiptoe to wake her,
her sleepy eyes lighting up when she saw me.

We'd water the garden together,
her giggles filling the morning air,
her tiny hands gripping the hose
as she splashed more than she watered.

Then, it was her, our husky, and me to the park.
I'd carry her laughter back with me like a trophy,
even as you called out, *"Don't take too long!"*
But we always did, our stolen moments
are too precious to cut short.

By the time we returned,
you'd be waiting, arms crossed,
mock scolding us for always running late.
She'd duck behind me, her little giggles infectious,
and I'd grin and whisper back to her,
"Mommy looks cutie when she's angry, doesn't she?"

And we'd rush through breakfast,
her calling for you to braid her hair,
you stomping over with half-feigned frustration,
scolding us both for our tardiness.

But somehow, we'd make it.
Her, you, me, all of us
tumbling into the car, late, but together,
ready to face another day of the life we built.

And Sundays were ours.
A Little piece of the week we carved out just for us,
a day that felt like a reset,
a chance to breathe together.
We'd head to the city, the bustling streets
full of people we didn't know,
but we didn't need to know them,
'cause we had each other.

We'd start at the mall, wandering, hand in hand,
me stealing glances at you when you didn't notice,
catching that soft smile 'nd excitement,
that only I knew.

The hum of the crowd, the flashing lights,
all faded into the background as we walked,
the rhythm of our steps syncing,
as if we had our own beat,
our own little world that no one else could touch.

We'd stop at the food court,
the smell of popcorn and burgers thick in the air.
Our daughter would beg for candy,
and I'd be the soft one, letting her pick a treat
while you rolled your eyes,
grumbling about how she didn't need it.

But it didn't matter, because she'd look at you
with those eyes that always made you give in,
you'd sigh and buy her the biggest bag of sweets.

Then, maybe we'd catch a movie.
Something light, something silly, but still,
we'd sit there, shoulders touching,
laughing at jokes that weren't that funny,
but felt like they mattered because we were together.
Her giggles beside us would fill the dark theatre.

And sometimes, when the day was still young,
we'd take a detour, not straight home,
but to your parents' house.

I'd drop you and our daughter off,
kissing you both goodbye,
before heading to my mum's place,
just for a little while. Because I knew
you wouldn't be comfortable at mine.

You and her would stay,
filling your parents' house with love and noise,
and I'd visit mine, because that's what we did,
we shared our worlds.

But she would often beg to come with me
to my mum's, and I'd take her,
because it was important for her
to know both sides of her story,
to see where I came from,
to understand the roots of her family.

And when she wasn't with me,
she was with you, spending time with her
grandparents, creating her own memories.

Then, as the day wound down,
we'd come back together again,
You, me, her, our family whole.
No matter how the day unfolded,
it always ended with us,
a moment of quiet joy that felt like home,
wherever we were.

***

Dummy, this is what I dreamed for us. A life so rich in its simplicity that it didn't need the world's applause. But baby, it never happened. It never even began. You left before we could build it, before her tiny hands clung to mine, before her laughter filled the air. You left before the fights about the dog, before the dinners, before the mornings where I'd kiss you like it was the very first time.

A life that was never lived, just imagined, a future where everything was perfect, but it's all just a dream. We didn't get that life, baby. It was mine to hold, mine to imagine, but you left before I could even see if we could make it.

You left before I could prove that all those dreams could have been real, that all that love we talked about could've actually lived, that we could've had that house, that car, that backyard where our daughter ran free, and I could've taught her everything.

I dreamed of waking up to those mornings, waking up beside you, hearing our daughter's laughter fill the air, seeing us all grow old together. But it's just a thought now, a ghost of a future that will never come.

I'll never know if we would've made it, if we could've had that family, if I could've been the dad I dreamed of being, if we could've made those Sundays ours.
I'll never get to see that life unfold.
I'll never get the chance to prove that dream was real.

Because you left. And now I'm left with a story that's only in my head, a story that'll never see the light of day, a life that I'll never live. I can only hold onto the pieces, the "what ifs" and "maybes", but they'll never be more than just that. You took everything with you when you left. My future, my hopes, my dreams.

And I'm here, stuck with nothing but the ache of never getting to see if this life was even possible. But damn, baby, I would've loved it. I would've loved it with you.
But now, it's just me and this dream,
a dream that'll never come true.

Seasons,

Yeah, they told me that love would stay, that it was
something divine,
a place where I could rest, something I could believe
in,
but no one warned me how quietly it can change,
how it shifts beneath your feet before you can even
see the cracks.
It doesn't vanish in some dramatic, fiery way;
it erodes, piece by piece, turning into something you
can't hold,
something you can't even recognize anymore.

You feel it first in the silences, in the way their words
grow soft,
not tender, but distant, as if love has forgotten how to
speak.
And you tell yourself it's nothing, just a phase that
passes by,
but deep down, your heart knows, it's slipping away.
Love doesn't scream when it dies, it whispers,
it lingers just enough to make you believe it's still
there,
and then it's gone, leaving you clutching at emptiness.

I thought I could keep it, thought if I gave enough of
myself,
I could make it stay, hold it steady, keep it from turning
cold.

But love isn't yours to keep, no matter how tightly you
cling.

It moves just like the seasons, indifferent to what it
leaves behind,
and when it goes, it takes pieces of you with it,
pieces you'll never get back, no matter how hard you
try.

And the worst part? The worst part is that love
changes
before it leaves, like a stranger slipping into familiar
skin.
You look at them, and for a moment, they're still there,
but something is off, something you can't quite name.
It eats at you, the not knowing, the way they smile
like they're already gone, like you're the last to realize
you've been holding onto someone who isn't holding
on to you.

I thought love was steady, that it would never let go,
but it let go so quietly, I didn't even feel it slip away.
And now I'm here, trying to make sense of the ruins,
of the life we built that's now just rubble and dust.
I keep asking myself if it was ever real,
or if I just imagined it all,
if love was only ever a dream I made myself believe in.

But that's the truth of love, isn't it?
It changes, it fades, it forgets what it once was,
and it leaves you standing in the aftermath,

holding the pieces of something you thought would
last forever.
Love doesn't wait for you to catch up,
doesn't hold your hand while it walks away.
It moves like the seasons,
and you're just another casualty of its passing.

What was I holding onto?

I thought love was the one thing that couldn't fail me,
the one place in the world where I could finally just be,
with no masks, no defences, no fear of falling apart.
I thought if I gave you everything, you'd hold my heart
like it mattered, like it was something worth keeping
safe,
but instead, you… you just dropped it, like it was too
much to take.
And now I'm here, staring at these pieces, wondering
why
I still can't hate you, even though you didn't even try.

Do you know what it's like to pour your soul into
someone,
to strip yourself bare and hand over everything you've
done,
every dream, every pain and every hidden fear?
Do you know what it's like to trust someone enough to
let them near,
only to watch them walk away without so much as a
glance back?
I gave you my light, my everything, and you left me in
the black.
Now I'm stuck here, replaying every word you ever
said,
trying to figure out which one of them was real, or if it's
all in my head.

I remember how your voice used to feel like home,

how every "I love you" felt carved into stone.
But it wasn't, was it? It was just dust in the fleeting wind,
scattered by time, by life, by whatever excuse you pinned
on the wall when you told yourself that you had to go.
Did you even feel it, the weight of leaving me so damn low?
Or was I just collateral, a casualty of your path,
someone you outgrew, left behind in your aftermath?

I can't stop asking myself if I wasn't enough,
if my love was too soft, or maybe too rough.
Was it the way I held you, too tight, too desperate,
trying to keep something alive that was already desolate?
Or was it just you, finding a reason to leave,
because staying was harder than making me grieve?
I don't know, and I hate that I'll never understand
why you let go when I was reaching for your hand.

Do you even think about me? Do you ever feel this ache?
Or am I the only one lying here, breaking for a love you faked?
I hate that I care, that I still wonder if you're okay,
if you've found what you were looking for when you walked away.
And I hate myself for loving you, for holding onto the past,
for clinging to memories of something that was never built to last.

I hate that I gave you so much of me, so much I can't
get back,
and now I'm left with this emptiness, this endless
lack.

They say time heals, but what the hell does that even
mean?
Does it make the nights less lonely, the spaces in
between
the moments where your face still flashes in my mind?
Does it erase the way your voice still echoes, unkind in
the silence where I used to feel your breath?
Because if this is healing, it feels a lot like death.
And maybe that's what love is, in the end,
a slow, quiet death that masquerades as a friend,
promising forever while it sharpens its knife,
leaving you bleeding out in the wreckage of your life.

I don't believe in love anymore; how could I?
When the one thing I trusted became the reason I cry?
When the hands I held turned into the ones that let go,
and the person I loved became someone I don't
know?
I want to move on, I want to let this all go,
but how do you bury something that still refuses to
decompose?
How do you forget someone who lives in your veins,
whose absence feels like poison, coursing through
your pain?

I don't have answers, just questions that won't stop.

I don't have closure, I'm stuck in this endless drop
into a void I didn't know existed before.

And maybe that's the real truth of love, it's a war
you don't always win, a battle you lose with grace,
a choice to give someone the power to take your
place.
And when they leave, you're left with the pieces,
trying to figure out how to breathe while the ache
increases.

I hope one day you understand what you've done,
not because I want you to hurt, but because I want you
to run
out of excuses for why you couldn't stay.
I want you to look in the mirror and see the weight of
that day
when you chose to leave, when you let us fall apart,
when you broke the one person who gave you their
heart.
But even then, I know it won't fix this hole in my chest,
this gaping wound where love was supposed to rest.

And here I am, writing this, because I don't know what
else to do.
I can't scream, I can't cry, I can only write the truth.
And the truth is, I loved you with everything I had,
and losing you has been the kind of pain that drives
you mad.
But I'm still here, broken and bleeding,
waiting for the day when my heart stops pleading
for someone who's never coming back.

Seventeen,

Seventeen winters, and it feels so wrong,
like I've lived too little, but I've been here too long.
Another year older, but what have I gained?
Only scars on my soul, only tears that remain.

What is a birthday but a cruel little lie,
a marker of time meant to pass me by?
There's no joy in the candles, no spark in the flame,
just smoke in my lungs and the weight of my name.

Seventeen years, and what do I see?
A hollow-eyed stranger staring right back at me.
The boy I once was, now buried and gone,
and the man I've become is a life gone wrong.

What am I, but a breathing regret?
A body that moves, a mind drowning in debt,
not the kind you can pay with coins or gold,
but the kind that haunts you, that never grows old.

A Love and now it's gone, like a whisper in wind,
she saw all my cracks, all the ways I'd sinned.
Her eyes turned cold, her touch grew thin,
I tried to hold on, but I couldn't win.
Her love was a flame I burned through too fast,
now I'm haunted by her shadows that trespass.

Friends, what friends? When I couldn't make them
stay,

no matter how much I gave away.
I tried to be enough, but I fell apart in every dispart,
guess I'm not someone who can hold a heart.
I can't make them happy; I'm not what they need,
not worth their time, not worth the seed.

My mother, her disappointment, sharpest of all
blades,
cutting me deeper with each grade I've made.
Her eyes, they search for a light in my face,
but all it finds is this desolate empty space.
Her silence is louder than her words ever could be,
and it screams, *"Is this really the son meant for me?"*

Seventeen years, and my name tastes like ash,
my dreams are in ruins, my hopes a crash.
I've seen the bottom, I've kissed the abyss,
and it swallowed me whole, left me with this.

I can't be the hero my sister deserves,
can't guide her, protect her, steady her nerves.
She looks up to me, but I can't even stand,
like an erratic foundation in the house built on sand.

What's left for me now? A future unknown,
a road with no signs, a path overgrown.
Higher studies? A blur, a shadow, a void,
a dream I can't touch and a hope that's destroyed.
What job, what career, what life will I make,
when everything I touch just seems to bend and
break?

Seventeen folds, and the failure runs deep,
in my veins, in my heart, in the dreams I can't keep.
I carry it with me, this heavy disease,
a weight on my chest, a wound that won't cease.

What am I supposed to do with this pain?
What am I supposed to learn from the rain?
If life is a lesson, then teach me why,
I was born just to stumble and crawl and cry.

Seventeen years, and my world feels so small,
I'm not climbing; I've fallen and shattered it all.
The dreams I once held are nothing but dust,
and the stars in my eyes have turned into rust.

But maybe this is the way it must be,
To break so completely, to finally see
that life isn't kind, it never plays fair,
It doesn't stop spinning for the weight that you bear.

And yet, I still breathe, though I don't know why,
I still drag my body under this heavy sky.
Maybe one day, one day I'll find a reason,
But for now, I'm just weathering the season.

Seventeen winters, and this is my truth,
a life full of rubble, a burned-out youth.
But if pain is my fuel, then let it ignite,
I'll bleed these words, as I write through the night.

Dear god,

Dear God, they say it's 2025, a chance to start anew,
but how can I... when I've lost the map that leads to
you?
The fireworks lit the sky; I saw the colours blaze and
die,
is that what I am, a fleeting burst in the empty sky?

What could I have been if I'd chased the dreams I left
behind?
Would I have been someone stronger, someone less
confined?
Why did I let these scars carve silence into my name?
Why does it feel like I'm the only one carrying this
shame?

If I hadn't burned those bridges, would I have found my
way?
If I'd chosen the right words, would they still have
stayed?
Am I a prisoner of the choices I can never undo?
Could I have been free, walking hand in hand with
You?

What would it feel like to wake up and not dread the
day ahead?
What would it mean to carry hope instead of the
weight of things unsaid?
If I'd made better choices, could my heart have been
whole

or am I destined to be this shadow, tethered to a
fractured soul?

Why does every good thing feel like it was meant for
someone else?
Why do I tear down bridges instead of asking for help?
Would I be happier if I'd let people stay instead of
pushing them away
or was I always meant to lose, to watch the light
decay?

If I'd held on tighter, would love have saved me from
the fall?
If I'd let go sooner, would I feel anything at all?
Why do I carry my agony like a torch in the night,
when I know it's the very thing that blinds my sight?

Do You hear me, God, or am I shouting at the sky?
Am I searching for answers in a silence that won't
reply?
If I had been braver, would my reflection look back
with pride
or am I forever bound to the wreckage I hide?

Do You remember the promises I whispered when I
was young?
Did You keep track of the dreams I buried before
they'd begun?
If I asked You now, would you give me the strength to
forgive
or is redemption a gift for those who truly know how to
live?

Why does the past feel closer than the future ever
could?
Why do I fear the good things, like I'm unworthy of
what's good?

Do You ever look at me, God, and wonder what went
wrong
or am I just another lost soul, humming a broken song?

Why does regret feel heavier than the life I failed to
chase?
Why do I find comfort in the emptiness I embrace?
If I turned around now, could I walk into the light
or would the weight of my mistakes pull me back into
the night?

If I'd chosen differently, would I know what warmth
feels like?
If I'd walked a different path, would I have found the
will to fight?
Do You think I'm strong, or do You see how weak I've
become?
Do You know how it feels to carry regret that weighs
like a ton?

What would I have seen if I'd lifted my eyes back then?
Would I have known joy, or was it always pretend?
Do You see the cracks in the soul I try to disguise?
Do You hear the questions buried in my midnight
cries?

Could I have been someone whose words built
something bright,
Instead of a scribe who only writes at the wake of the
night?
Would my hands have created instead of torn apart,
If I had let your light shine instead of guarding my
heart?

Why does the gap between what is and what could be,
stretch wider than any ocean, swallowing me?
Why do I cling to the pain like it's all I'll ever know,
when I could've let You guide me where I needed to
go?

Why does it feel like the me I could've been, is
haunting this room?
Why do I hold onto failure like it's a song I have to
croon?
If You could rewrite me, would You erase all my scars
or are they the only proof I have of who we are?

God, if I let these questions linger, will they consume
me whole
or are they the breadcrumbs that might lead me back
to my soul?
If I dare to believe I'm more than my scars and sin,
could I rise from the ashes of who I've been?

It's January 21ˢᵗ,

I don't even know why I'm sitting here and writing this.
It's not like you'll ever read it,
not like you'll care, not like you ever cared enough to
stay.
But, the words won't stop clawing their way out of me,
and my heart feels like it's choking on your name.

Did you know today was supposed to matter?
It's January twenty-first, it's our... our first anniversary.
Do you even know what that supposed to mean?
Or did you throw that away along with everything else,
like I was just another thing you didn't have time for?

Do you remember when we promised to fight for this?
To fight for us?
I would've walked through fire for you,
but you, you couldn't even bother to stay long enough
to hold my hand.

What was it, really... The school? Grade twelve?
Is that what made you chose this path, to leave?
Because, what, suddenly school mattered more than
the life we built together?
Didn't you know a year ago what this year would bring?
Or was I just too blind to see the lies in your eyes
when you said we'd make it through anything?

Tell me, did you plan this all along? Did you sit there
and calculate

the exact moment you'd break me in two,
when I was too far gone in love with you to save
myself?

Was it fun, watching me crumble,
watching me cling to a future you'd already walked
away from?
Did you laugh at how easily I fell for your lies,
how I believed you when you said we had forever?

I... I gave you my everything.
My time, my trust, my heart, my soul.
I built us a future, brick by brick,
laying down every piece of my heart as the foundation,
believing you were doing the same.
But you, you just tore it all down, without a second
thought,
and left me standing in the ruins,
asking myself what the hell I did to deserve this.

Do you even feel guilty?
Does it ever cross your mind, the way you gutted me,
the way you walked away without even looking back?
Do you feel anything at all, or was it always this easy
for you
to discard people who gave you their whole goddamn
world?
Because I gave you mine, and you just shattered it.
And left me here, drowning in the pieces,
while you walked off into the next chapter of your life
like none of this ever mattered.

How do you live with yourself, knowing what you've
done to me?
How do you even sleep at night,
knowing that the promises you made are still keeping
me awake?

You told me you loved me, did you even mean it?
Or was that just another pretty thing to say,
another lie to keep me hanging on a little longer?
Because I can't believe you could ever love someone
and still hurt them like this.

What kind of person does that?
What kind of person builds a life with someone,
brick by brick, hand in hand,
only to tear it all down when it gets a little hard?
What kind of person tells someone that they're their
forever,
then decides that forever is just too long?

You didn't even fight for us.
You didn't even dare to try.
You... you just gave up, like I was nothing,
like we were nothing,
like I never meant a damn thing to you.

Do you know what it feels like to live with that?
To wake up every day and wonder why I wasn't
enough?
Why my love wasn't enough?
Why you couldn't stay, even though I begged you to?

Do you know what it feels like to carry the weight of a
future that'll never exist
to live every day in the shadow of what we could've
been?
Because that's what you left me with.
That's the legacy of your love.

I hope you're happy now.
I hope you've found whatever it was you thought
was more important than me, than us.
I hope you never have to feel what I'm feeling right
now,
because it's unbearable.
It's more than the hell.
And I wouldn't wish this kind of pain on anyone,
not on you, any day.

But then again, maybe... maybe you deserve it.
Maybe one day, you'll find someone you love
as much as I loved you,
and maybe they'll leave you, stranded, empty-handed.
Maybe they'll rip your heart out the way you ripped out
mine,
and maybe then, you'll finally understand
what you did to me.

But even then, I don't think you'll get it.
Because you just don't care, do you?
You never did.
And that's the part that hurts the most,
knowing that I loved you with everything I had,
and it still wasn't enough to make you stay.

And here I am, on what should've been our
anniversary,
writing this, bleeding this, breaking over you again.
And you?
You're probably out there living your best life,
completely oblivious to the wreckage you left behind.
I hope it was worth it.
I hope I was worth leaving.
But the truth is, I don't think I'll ever know.

I keep asking why, why it had to be me,
why you could walk away so easily while I stayed
behind,
haunted by the echoes of your promises,
by the future we built in whispers and dreams,
by the life we swore would never crumble.
Was I that forgettable? That replaceable?
Do you ever feel it too, this emptiness you left in your
wake?
Or is it just me, standing here with nothing but ghosts
for company?

But even as I write these words, dripping with
bitterness,
I can't shake this feeling that I'm being unfair.
How do I hate you when my heart still calls for you in
the dark?
When your absence still cuts deeper than I care to
admit?
Maybe it's not you I'm angry at, maybe it's myself.
For loving too much, for holding on too tightly,
for making you the villain in a story where we both lost.

I didn't want to write this, didn't want to turn you into
someone you were never meant to be.
But here I am, spilling everything,
like it'll somehow ease the ache of not knowing why.

Ugh, baby, why? Why did it have to be this way?
I want to hate you, God, I really want to, but I just
can't.

I can't even summon the strength to despise you,
even after everything you've done.
I feel like hating myself for writing about you like this,
so cruel, so unfair. But then again,
wasn't it cruel to leave me like you did?
And yet, I know you must have had your reasons,
I know you must've carried your own pain,
but you could've told me, couldn't you?
You could've trusted me enough to explain.
Was I not worth that? Not even a single moment of
honesty?
I always wanted what was best for you, baby,
and if leaving me was what you needed to soar,
I would've let you go. I swear I would've,
even though it would've shattered me all the same.

It's cruel, isn't it?
Writing about you like this, tearing you apart in my
head,
when I know... I *know* that you must have had your
reasons.

I know you weren't trying to break me for fun,
but couldn't you have let me know why?
Did I not deserve even that?
A whisper of truth? A sliver of closure?
How is it that I loved you with everything I had,
but not enough to warrant a proper goodbye?

I'm sorry, I'm sorry for the anger, for the words I threw
like daggers,
for the questions that were meant to hurt more than to
heal.
It's not that I wanted to paint you as the villain.
I just didn't know how else to survive this pain.
Because deep down, I know you're not cruel.
You're not heartless.
You were just… lost.
And maybe I was, too.

But couldn't we have been lost together?
I would've held your hand through the chaos,
through every storm that this life threw at us,
through every late-night doubt and every tear-streaked
fear.
We could've made it, baby.
Don't you think?
Or was I just fooling myself,
believing in a version of us that only existed in my
mind?

Ugh, I hate myself for this, for still defending you in my
head,
for still imagining that you had no choice,

that you must've been drowning, too.
I tell myself that if you could've stayed, you would
have.
That if you had found the words to explain,
you would've told me why you had to leave.
But instead, I'm left here with silence.
With questions that only echo louder the more I try to
bury them.

Do you know how much I wanted to fight for you?
Do you know how much I *still* want to?
Even now, after all this, I'd take your hand
and tell you we'll figure it out, whatever it is, together.
Because that's all I ever wanted:
to be by your side, to be your safe place,
to see you soar even if it meant staying behind to
cheer you on.

But you didn't give me the chance, did you?
You didn't trust me enough to let me in.
You didn't believe in us enough to think we could
weather this storm.
And that's what cuts the deepest, not the leaving,
but the fact that you didn't think I was strong enough
to carry you when you needed me most.

I just hate that I'm still writing about you,
that every line I carve into this page feels like another
wound,
another way of bleeding for someone
who doesn't even think about me anymore.

But baby, I just can't help it.
Because even after all the hurt,
after all the ways you've left me in ruins,
I still love you.

God, how pathetic is that?
How stupid am I to sit here,
still holding onto the ghost of you,
still searching for pieces of us in the wreckage,
still hoping that maybe, just maybe,
you'll read this someday and know that I never
stopped caring?

I always wanted what was best for you,
and if leaving me was what you needed to do,
I would've let you go.
I would've cried, and screamed, and fallen apart,
but I would've let you go, knowing it was what you
needed.
All you had to do was tell me, baby.
All you had to do was let me in.

But you didn't.
You left me here with nothing but questions,
with a love that feels more like a curse than a gift,
with memories that burn, instead of comfort.
And yet, I still can't bring myself to hate you.
I still can't stop myself from loving the person
who made me feel alive in a way no one else ever has.

Now I am... I'm writing this mess of a poem,
not knowing how to end it, not knowing how to stop.
Because how do you stop loving someone
who was your entire world,
even when they've walked away from you?
How do you let go of that one person
you thought would never leave?

Maybe I'll never know.
Maybe I'll spend the rest of my life writing about you,
trying to make sense of the pain,
trying to find a way to forgive myself for loving you so
much.

Or maybe not, I... I don't want to...

But if this is what love feels like,
if this is what it means to have your heart ripped apart
and still beat for the one who tore it into oblivion,
then maybe love isn't meant to be kind.
And maybe that's the cruellest truth of all.

After all this time,

Can you just hold me tonight, though the air feels thin,
though the warmth of your hands never touches my
skin?
Wrap me in your whispers, your breath, a trace,
let me pretend there's still life in this desolate space.
The stars look on, so lifeless, hollow and still,
as though they've watched me bend to your will.
And the moon, half-lost, and won't speak your name
as it has learned, just like me, the rules of this game.

Lie if you must, as my ears crave your sound,
say you'll be back when the world comes around.
Say that this fracture was meant to mend,
that all broken paths were meant to find their end.
I'll wait in the ruins where our love once burned,
where the laughter faded and shadows turned.
I'll wait where the sky collapses into blue,
where time forgets, but I'll always remember you.

I've been cold, since the day you went black,
since the clock froze hands, it can't take back.
I don't know who I've become tonight,
a man of stone, or a ghost in flight.
But even if the dawn refuses to rise,
and even if silence swallows the skies,
I'll search the void for what can't be seen,
'a flicker of you' in the in-between.

If we met again where shadows bled,
would you still remember the words I said?
Would you know the weight I bore,
the love I carried, the ache I wore?
'Cause I'd know you, through veils and through flame,
through shapes that shift and masks unnamed.
I'd find you where the lost ones tread,
Where love isn't spoken, where it's felt instead.

Just... just hold me again, though your hands aren't
near,
even as the memories sharpens to spears.
Even as touch turns fleeting and thin,
let me feel the ghost of where you've been.
Let me believe this hollow is whole,
let me cradle what's left of my soul.
Because even in my dreams, the edges fray,
and the light you were, still slips away.

If you could see what I've become,
would you still claim the man I run from?
Would you trace my scars like a map to the past,
or leave them untouched, let the moments last?
Because I would hold you, through fire and frost,
through every breath that this body has lost.
I'd cling to the shadow you leave behind,
a tether to what I'll never tend to find.

And even if this world unravels whole,
If time itself devours this aching soul,
I'd still wait in the fragments, the shattered and worn,
for the echo of you where hearts are torn.
So just hold me tonight, just a word, a spark,
a flicker of warmth in this endless dark.
Even if you've gone, burying me half-dead,
your name still burns where the living once bled.

If you ever see this,

Hey baby, it's been a long time, hasn't it? Been a long
time since I heard your voice,
since I last stood close enough to you to listen, yet still
felt miles apart by choice.
Since we last spoke, since we last locked eyes
without looking away like strangers,
since I last saw you and didn't feel my heart pull
between love and anger.

I guess we'll never speak again, not like we used to,
not like before,
because if time has taught me one thing, it's that some
doors close and stay closed forevermore.

And today, of all days, I saw you again, right in front of
me, breathing the same air,
February 27th, 2025, the day of our chemistry board
exam, the day I knew you'd be there.
The day everything we worked for was laid out on
paper, blue ink on a blank slate,
but maybe, in some twisted way, it was also the day I
realized that I started to accept fate.

You were sitting two rows ahead of me, lost in your
own mind like you always are,
and even without looking at you directly, I could tell,
you weren't nervous, not even by far.
Of course, you weren't. You've always been like that,

always had that sharp focus in your eyes,
like you already knew all the answers, like you never
had to second-guess or analyze.
And baby, that's what made me fall for you, that's
what made me believe,
that if I stood beside you long enough, maybe I'd learn
to carry my heart on my sleeve.

Then the bus stopped, and you walked off, fast, with
your friends, disappearing into the crowd,
and I stood there for a second, staring after you,
feeling something new but not saying it out loud.
It wasn't pain, it wasn't longing, it wasn't that deep
ache I used to carry in my chest,
it was just... warmth. A quiet kind of peace, like
maybe, just maybe, this was for the best.

The exam started, three whole hours of equations and
chemical formulas blurred in my mind,
and somehow by god's grace, I didn't leave a single
question behind.

And when it was over, I walked outside to the ground
where everyone would meet, and let myself breathe,
and there you were again, walking by, laughing, your
happiness like a melody I'll never unweave.
You didn't see me. You didn't look. You were too
caught up in your own world,
and for the first time in eight months, I didn't feel my
stomach twist, didn't feel my heart unfurl.

And that's when I knew.

Maybe I'm finally letting go.
Maybe the weight I've been carrying isn't as heavy as it
was before.
Maybe, for the first time in forever, I don't need you to
love me anymore.

And baby, I just want to say... Thank you.

This year has been everything, more than I ever
thought I'd feel,
like I've lived a thousand lifetimes in just these
months, highs and lows spinning like a wheel.
I've made friends who feel like family, I've lost love
that felt like home,
I've sat in silence with grief, I've danced with
heartbreak, I've learned what it means to be alone.
I've smiled so wide it felt like I could swallow the sun,
and I've cried so hard I thought my body would come
undone.
I've been broken, I've been whole, I've been
somewhere in between,
and through it all, baby, you were there, even when
you weren't, you were still seen.

I still think about the day you told me you loved me,
the day we first spoke like we were meant to,
it was like the universe had written our story long
before we even knew.
Like every single moment since seventh grade was
building up to this,
like fate had aligned itself to make sure we'd never
miss.

And it felt so damn right, didn't it? For a while, it felt like forever,
like no matter what happened, we'd always find our way back together.

And I won't lie to you, I thought you were my last, my only, my always,
I thought we'd make it through every storm, hold on through all the dark days.
So I made you my world, closed every other window, gave you every part of me,
but now I see, baby, that love isn't about losing yourself for someone else's need.

And yet, I still wonder, if we had just played our roles right,
if we had met at a different time, if we had fought a little harder, held on a little tight,
if we had swallowed our pride instead of letting silence stretch between us like an endless road,
if we had chosen to understand instead of assume,if we had carried the weight instead of letting it explode,
if we had just looked at each other one last time with love instead of doubt,

would we have made it? Would we have found a way to turn this all around?
Would we have been something more, something unshakable, something built to last?
Would we have been the couple that laughed at the storms, that never let go of the past?

Because baby, I swear, I used to believe in us like a prayer whispered in the dark,
I used to think no matter how hard life hit, we'd always find a way back to the start.

But maybe I was a fool, maybe we were young,
maybe I thought timing was just an excuse and that effort could change our weight.
Because if I'm being honest, we could have made it,
I know that. I feel that in my bones.
But *"could have"* and *"did"* are two different things,
and no matter how much I think about it, I'm standing here alone.

Maybe it was timing. Maybe it was fate.
Maybe we were a masterpiece left unfinished, a song that never got to its final state.
Maybe we were never meant to last, just meant to meet,
meant to love each other just enough to know what heartbreak truly means.

Because I swear, baby, I would have given you the world if you had just asked,
I would have held on so tight, I would have made this love our very last.
But love isn't a one-man fight, isn't something one person can hold together,
it takes two, it takes effort, it takes a promise that doesn't wither under pressure.

And yet, even now, even after all this time,
if you came to me, if you held my hand, if you
whispered, "I need you to be mine,"
I swear, I'd still run to you like I always did,
I'd still take your hand, still follow wherever you went,
no matter what life forbid.
Because these emotions don't die, they just stay
quiet, waiting in the back of your soul,
some of them are stubborn, refusing to let go, even
when you know you should let them go.

But I know, baby, I know... this isn't one of those
stories with a surprise twist,
there's no last-minute realization, no fate intervening,
no final kiss.
You're not coming back, and deep down, I've
accepted that truth,
even if a part of me still aches, still wonders, still
clings to the "what ifs" of me and you.

And that's okay I guess.
Because love doesn't have to end in forever to be real,
it doesn't have to be a lifetime to matter, doesn't have
to be a promise we still feel.

Sometimes love is just a chapter, just a lesson, just a
season we get to keep,
and baby, I'll keep this one close, even if it only lives in
my memories, deep.

I won't blame you, I won't hate you, I won't pretend it
didn't mean the world,

I won't erase the late-night talks, the way you laughed, the way you stared,
into my eyes like I was the safest place you had ever known,
I won't erase the way we loved, even if now, I stand alone.

So baby, just... Thank You. For the love, for the lesson, for the laughter and the pain,
for the memories that shine like gold and the ones that sting like acid rain.
for being the first to show me what love feels like at its highest and its worst,
for the moments I'll cherish even when time keeps pulling us further apart.

Your name's still saved, ringtone's still the same,
just a tiny, stupid reminder of a love that once had my name.
I want this to be a lifeline which is meant for you to call,
anytime, any day, no matter what. No questions, no walls.
And it's your favorite song that'll play whenever your name lights my screen,
even though I know you won't call, and maybe you never will again.

And baby, I wish I could tell you all of these,
I wish I could sit across from you, look you in the eyes, and just let it exist,
every feeling, every thought, every unsaid word,

but I know I can't, I know you've moved on, and maybe
I should too, undeterred.

So instead, I write.
I let these words spill, I carve them into this page,
let them sit here, quiet and waiting, frozen in time,
untouched by age.
Because I can't say them to you, can't whisper them
into the space between us,
but maybe, just maybe, someday, these words will
find their way to where you are,
maybe you'll pick up this book, maybe you'll flip to the
last page,
and for a moment, just a moment, you'll remember
everything we were, everything we gave.

Maybe you'll hear my voice in these lines,
maybe you'll feel the weight of what I could never say
in time.
And maybe it won't change anything, maybe it'll just
be a passing thought,
but if it makes you pause, if it makes you remember,
even for a second,
then that's enough, that's all I ever really sought.

So I leave this here,
a testament to my love, wrapped in words, laid bare
just for you, just for us, just for the love that still lingers
in my chest.

Thank you, **Dummy**.
For everything.

9 798889 744304